LIVES OF
Vo

Modern Saints
Revised Edition

Written by Bart Tesoriero
Illustrations by Michael Adams

TABLE OF CONTENTS

Library of Congress Control Number: 2012905936
ISBN 978-1-61796-051-2

SAINT FRANCIS DE SALES

Feast Day: January 24

Patron of Writers and Journalists

Saint Francis was born to a noble French family in 1567. He loved studies, and he earned doctorates from the University of Padua in both canon and civil law. Even more than studies, Francis loved God, because he knew that God loved him. He became a priest in 1593, and later became the bishop of Geneva. Saint Francis de Sales preached and wrote with great zeal. Through leaflets and books he had written, many people returned to the Church, and many faithful remained. As a result, Francis is remembered today as the patron of writers and the Catholic press.

Saint Francis de Sales died in 1622 and was canonized in 1653. In 1877, he was declared a Doctor of the Church.

Prayer to Saint Francis de Sales for Writers

Dear Saint Francis, out of your great love for God, you allowed yourself to be used as the instrument of His Word. Help all writers and journalists to copy your holy example of giving yourself to God. Dear God, through the prayers of Saint Francis de Sales, help all of us to think well, write well, and love well. In Jesus' name we pray. Amen.

Saint Francis de Sales, pray for us.

SAINT ROSE OF LIMA

Feast Day: August 23

Patron of Florists and Gardeners

Isabel Flores de Oliva was born in Lima, Peru, in 1586. She was so lovely that her parents called her Rose. Rose grew more beautiful and more in love with Jesus ever day.

Rose joined the Dominican Third Order in 1606, at age 20, and gave herself as a virgin to Christ. She lived alone in the family garden, raising vegetables and serving the poor and sick.

God gave Rose visions and blessings, and she also suffered in her body, soul, and spirit. God increased His love in her heart as she offered herself to Him. Saint Rose of Lima died at the age of 31 in 1617.

Prayer to Saint Rose of Lima

Dear Saint Rose, you loved God with all your heart, with all your body, and with all your mind. Please bless those who bring joy to others as florists and gardeners. Dear God, through the prayers of Saint Rose help us to please You always and to be kind to others. In Jesus' name. Amen.

Saint Rose of Lima, pray for us.

SAINT MARTIN DE PORRES

Feast Day: November 3

Patron of Barbers

Saint Martin de Porres was born at Lima, Peru, in 1579. His father was a Spanish knight and his mother a freed slave. When he was 15, Martin entered the Dominican Friary at Lima and served as a farm laborer and barber.

He cared for the poor, the sick, and the dying. God endowed Saint Martin with many graces, including humility, gentleness, wisdom, and healing. He opened many orphanages and raised money for children by begging on the streets.

Saint Martin de Porres loved all of God's creation, caring for dogs, cats, and other animals. He was a close friend of Saint Rose of Lima, and he died on November 3, 1639.

Prayer to Saint Martin de Porres for Hairdressers

Dear Saint Martin de Porres, no task was too small for you to perform with great love. Please pray for all barbers and hairdressers. Dear Lord, through the prayers of Saint Martin, bless all hairdressers who seek to make their clients and the world more beautiful. In Jesus' name we pray. Amen.

Saint Martin de Porres, pray for us.

SAINT VINCENT DE PAUL

Feast Day: September 27

Patron of Prisoners and the Poor

Saint Vincent de Paul was born in France in 1576. He was ordained a priest in 1600. A few years later, he was captured by Turkish pirates and sold into slavery. Saint Vincent escaped to France, where he brought the love and hope of Jesus to prisoners confined in the galleys. He served in a parish near Paris where he started groups to help the poor and forgotten, the sick, and those in need of work. He went through the streets of Paris at night, seeking the children who were left there to die. He founded orders of men and women to help the poor and afflicted, and to bring comfort to all. Saint Vincent de Paul died in 1660.

Prayer to Saint Vincent de Paul for Charity Workers

Dear Saint Vincent, you worked very hard to bring faith, hope, and charity to the poorest of the poor. Please pray that all who serve others will have the same zeal and compassion for the poor that you did. Dear God, through the prayers of Saint Vincent de Paul, please bless all who serve You in the poor and needy. Strengthen them that they may always see You in those they serve. In Jesus' name we pray. Amen.

Saint Vincent de Paul, pray for us!

SAINT LOUISE DE MARILLAC

Feast Day: March 15

Patron of Nurses and Social Workers

Saint Louise de Marillac was born in 1591 in Paris, France. Her mother died after her birth. In 1613, she married, and she and her husband, Antoine, bore a son. In 1625, after a long illness, Antoine died. While raising her son, Louise did many good works. Saint Francis de Sales became her confessor and spiritual director. Through Saint Francis, Louise met Saint Vincent de Paul. In 1633, they began together the Daughters of Charity. The women who served in this order cared for the homeless poor and for the needy children who lived in the streets.

Until her death in 1660, Saint Louise worked with all her might for the poor. She also helped her country to improve its social services for the poor. Today, Saint Louise de Marillac is recognized as the patron of social workers.

Prayer to Saint Louise for Nurses and Social Workers

Dear Saint Louise, you endured trials and challenges in your life, yet you used your talents to transform every one of them into a beautiful work for God. Please pray for all nurses and social workers, that they might feel Our Lord's great love in their hearts and then reach out to serve His children. Amen.

Saint Louise de Marillac, pray for us.

SAINT JOHN BAPTIST DE LA SALLE

Feast Day: April 7

Patron of Teachers

Saint John Baptist de la Salle was born in 1651 in France. He decided to follow Jesus at an early age, and became a priest in 1678. John wanted to help children learn better. In 1679, he helped a friend open up a school for poor boys. He realized that was what he wanted to do the rest of his life.

Saint John believed that the best way to serve his students was to teach their teachers. He therefore established the Institute of the Brothers of the Christian Schools in 1680. Soon after, he founded colleges for training teachers. John died in 1719, but his work spread quickly throughout the whole world. Pope Leo XIII canonized Saint John Baptist de la Salle in 1900, and in 1950 he was made the patron saint of teachers.

Prayer to Saint John Baptist de la Salle for Teachers

Dear Saint John Baptist de la Salle, you gave your life to educating the poorest members of the Church. Pray for all teachers to see Christ in their students and to live always for Him. Dear God, through the prayers of Saint John, please give Your Church good teachers today. In Jesus' name we pray. Amen.

Saint John Baptist de la Salle, pray for us.

SAINT KATERI TEKAKWITHA

Feast Day: July 14

Patron of the Environment

Tekakwitha — She who bumps into things — was born to a Mohawk warrior and a Christian mother in New York in 1656. Her parents died in a smallpox epidemic that left her with weakened eyes and a scarred face. Tekakwitha was living with her uncle and aunt when the Jesuit priests—the "Blackrobes"—came to her village. She told them that she wanted to be a Christian, and on Easter Sunday, 1676, Kateri (Catherine) Tekakwitha was baptized. Kateri left her family and traveled many miles to Canada, where she found refuge at the Saint Francis Xavier Mission. Kateri cared tenderly for children, the sick, and the elderly. After a long illness, she died in 1680. Pope John Paul II beatified Kateri, and on February 18, 2012, Pope Benedict XVI canonized Kateri Tekakwitha, the first Native American to be declared a Saint!

Prayer to Saint Kateri Tekakwitha for our Earth

Dear Saint Kateri, you loved God and all His creation. Please pray that all people will care for our earth. May we use the gifts of our earth to bring glory to God and good to others, especially the poor and suffering. Amen.

Saint Kateri Tekakwitha, pray for us!

SAINT GERARD

Feast Day: October 16

Patron of Expectant Mothers and Unborn Children

Saint Gerard was born in Italy in 1726. He joined the Redemptorist Order at the age of 23. Saint Gerard was obedient, pure, wise, and kind. God gave him gifts of healing and knowing what was in people's hearts.

Saint Gerard spent his life helping the needy and the poor. One day a pregnant mother was concerned about her unborn baby's health. She asked Gerard to pray for her. He did so and she gave birth to a healthy child! God worked many wonders through Saint Gerard. He died at the young age of 29, and was canonized in 1904. Saint Gerard is recognized today as the patron of expectant mothers and of safe delivery of children at birth.

Prayer to Saint Gerard for Mothers

Dear Saint Gerard, please pray for mothers and their unborn children, that God will bless them with the gift of life, grace, and peace. Dear God, the Giver of Life, through the prayers of Saint Gerard, please help mothers give birth to healthy children who will grow to love You and spread Your love to others. In Jesus' name. Amen.

Saint Gerard, pray for us.

SAINT ELIZABETH ANN SETON

Feast Day: January 4

Patron of Converts

Elizabeth Bayley was born in 1774 into an Episcopalian family. Her early life was quiet, simple, and often lonely. She loved to read the Bible and found great comfort in God's Word. Elizabeth married William Seton, but he died at an early age and left her with their five children. Elizabeth felt herself drawn to Christ in the Holy Eucharist, and she became a Roman Catholic in 1805. She founded the Sisters of Charity, beginning the American parochial school system. Mother Seton died in 1821, and became the first native-born American to be canonized!

Prayer to Saint Elizabeth Ann Seton for Converts

Dear Saint Elizabeth Ann Seton, you were a wife, a mother, a teacher, and the founder of a religious order. You became a Catholic because of your great love for Jesus in the most Blessed Sacrament. Please bless all who seek to know God as Catholics. Help them in their journey to a deeper faith, hope, and love. Dear God, through the prayers of Saint Elizabeth, give us all the grace to love You more, and to serve You with joy. In Jesus' name. Amen.

Saint Elizabeth Ann Seton, pray for us.

SAINT JOHN VIANNEY

Feast Day: August 4

Patron of Priests

Saint John Marie Vianney was born in France in 1786. He was ordained a priest in 1815 and sent to Ars, a little French village. He lived for his parishioners. He ate only a few potatoes and slept only a few hours every night, to win the graces of conversion for his parishioners. Thousands across the world came to him for confession and healing. The devil tormented Father Vianney, waking him at night with mocking voices, loud noises and even physical abuse, but Saint John Vianney kept very close to Jesus and Mary. He was so holy and good that even very evil sinners were converted at his mere word. Saint John Vianney died in 1859, and his body did not decay, but lies incorrupt to this very day. Pope Benedict XVI declared him the patron of all priests in 2009.

Prayer to Saint John Vianney for Priests

Dear Saint John Vianney, you were devoted to God and His people. Lord God, through the prayers of Saint John Vianney, please bless all priests. Help them to be holy and true. May they be bold and loving witnesses to the truth, and draw many to You. In Jesus' name we pray. Amen.

Saint John Vianney, pray for us!

SAINT JOHN NEUMANN

Feast Day: January 5

Patron of Catholic Education

Saint John Neumann was born in Bohemia in 1811. He left his home and traveled across the ocean to New York, where he was ordained a priest. Because there were so few priests in America, Father Neumann cared for 200,000 Catholics! He traveled from village to village, walking roads and climbing mountains to visit the sick, teach children, and celebrate Mass. Father Neumann joined the Redemptorists, a congregation dedicated to helping the poor and most abandoned. In 1852, he was ordained Bishop of Philadelphia. Bishop Neumann organized the first Catholic school system in the United States. He died in 1860. In 1977, Saint John Neumann became the first American bishop to be canonized!

Prayer to Saint John Neumann

O Saint John Neumann, you left your home and country to serve God. Please pray for all who teach others about the Catholic faith. Dear God, through the prayers of Saint John Neumann, help us also to serve those who are poor and suffering. Help us to be true to Jesus even when it is hard. In Jesus' name. Amen.

Saint John Neumann, pray for us.

SAINT BERNADETTE SOUBIROUS

Feast Day: April 16

Patron of the Sick

Bernadette Soubirous was born in Lourdes, France, in 1844. One day, as she was gathering firewood beside a river, Bernadette saw a beautiful Lady wearing a blue and white dress who was floating above a rose bush. The Lady smiled at her and made the sign of the cross with a golden rosary. Bernadette knelt down and began to pray. The Lady, who was the Virgin Mary, asked Bernadette to dig nearby. When she did so, a spring emerged with healing waters. Mary asked Bernadette to have a chapel built by the spot, so people could come there to wash and drink. The water from this spring continues to bring healings to many people. Our Lady also requested that a church be built there. Bernadette became a nun, and died a few years later. Pope Pius XI canonized Saint Bernadette in 1933.

Prayer to Saint Bernadette

Dear Saint Bernadette, thank you for being true to Mary, the Lady whom you saw, and to Jesus, her Son. Please pray for all who are ill or suffering. Dear God, through the prayers of Mother Mary and dear Saint Bernadette, please heal the sick in body and soul. In Jesus' name. Amen.

Saint Bernadette, pray for us.

SAINT THERESE OF LISIEUX

Feast Day: October 1

Patron of the Missions

Therese Martin was born in France in 1873. She was a happy child who loved Jesus. When her beloved mother died, young Therese became very ill, and she prayed to Mother Mary. Therese saw Mary smile at her and suddenly she was cured! She then became a Carmelite nun. Therese spent her life praying, helping priests, and sacrificing for souls. Loving and trusting in God, as a child, was her "little way" to Jesus. Her favorite saying was, "Love is repaid by love alone." Therese died at the age of 24, whispering, "My God, I love You!" Pope Pius XI canonized Saint Therese in 1925. Two years later, he named her the co-patron of the missions.

Prayer to Saint Therese for the Missions

Dear Saint Therese, you promised to spend your heaven doing good on earth. Please pray for all missionaries that they would always feel God's love and presence as they share His message. Dear God, through the intercession of Saint Therese, bless all who serve You in other lands. Keep them from all harm and reward them for their faithful service of You. In Jesus' name we pray. Amen.

Saint Therese of Lisieux, pray for us!

SAINT MAXIMILIAN KOLBE

Feast Day: August 14
Patron of Prisoners and Drug Addicts

Saint Maximilian Kolbe was born in 1894 in Poland and became a Franciscan priest. He founded the Immaculata Movement devoted to Our Lady. He used publications and a world-wide community to spread this devotion as far as Japan and India. In 1941, the Nazis arrested Father Kolbe and sent him to a prison camp in Auschwitz, Poland. A prisoner escaped, and the Nazis chose ten men to die as a warning to the others. Father Kolbe offered himself to die in the place of a young husband and father.

After two weeks without food or water, Father Kolbe was injected with acid, and died on August 14th, 1941. He is the patron of all those who struggle with addiction to drugs. In 1982 Pope John Paul II canonized Saint Maximilian Kolbe and declared him a martyr of love.

Prayer to Saint Maximilian Kolbe for Prisoners

Dear Saint Maximilian Kolbe, you loved others enough to die for them. Please help all who are in prison or who struggle with addiction to know the peace of God and the love of Mother Mary, who are always with them. Amen.

Saint Maximilian Kolbe, pray for us!

SAINT PIO OF PIETRELCINA

Feast Day: September 23

Patron of All who Suffer

Francesco Forgione was born in Italy, in 1887 and named in honor of Saint Francis. At an early age Francesco felt a deep love for Jesus and Mary, and he became a priest. He joined the Capuchins, a branch of the Franciscan Order, where he was known as Padre Pio. He suffered much, accepting it with praise and thanks to God, trusting that He could use it for the good of others. In 1918, Padre Pio received the stigmata—the wounds of Jesus—in his hands, feet, and side.

Padre Pio listened to confessions of people from all over for many hours every day. Through his prayers, thousands of sick people were healed. Padre Pio deeply loved Saint Michael, his guardian angel, and the souls in Purgatory. Padre Pio died in 1968, and in 2002, Pope John Paul II canonized him as Saint Pio of Pietrelcina!

Prayer to Saint Pio for the Sick

Dear Saint Pio, thank you for offering up your suffering for others. Please pray for all who are sick, especially my family or friends. May God bless and heal them. Amen.

Saint Pio, pray for us!

MODERN SAINTS

The past 500 years have brought trials and challenges for the Church and our world, but thankfully, "Jesus Christ is the same yesterday, today, and forever" (Hebrews 13:8).

In 1517, Christian Europe was divided by the Protestant Reformation. Saint Francis de Sales and others helped preach the enduring truths of Catholicism across France, Switzerland, and the continent. Saint Vincent de Paul and Saint Louise de Marillac worked selflessly caring for the poor and homeless, regardless of their religion, and helped countries develop new social services. They lived out the Bible truth that "faith without works is dead" (James 2:26). New religious orders like the Jesuits sailed the oceans and preached the Gospel to converts like Saint Kateri Tekakwitha, *the Lily of the Mohawks*, who joyfully received the Faith and were baptized.

Mother Mary appeared at Lourdes and Fatima, and Saint Maximilian Kolbe and others gave their lives in the face of tyrants and totalitarian regimes. Saints like Padre Pio helped people find healing in the compassion of Jesus.

Dear Modern Saints, you know what our world is like today. Help us to pray, hope, and to be not afraid. Jesus our Lord will never leave us nor forsake us. Come Lord Jesus! Amen.